SUMMA of

TOO MUCH AND NEVER ENOUGH

HOW MY FAMILY CREATED THE WORLD'S MOST DANGEROUS MAN

BY MARY L. TRUMP, PH.D

Proudly Brought To You By
Thomas Wade

ISBN: 978-1-952639-30-2

Table of Contents

EXECUTIVE SUMMARY

Donald Trump has a story, like many other people. Several books have been written about the President of the United States, but *Too Much And Never Enough* sits in a class of its own. This book takes the reader back in time, exposing and unraveling all that the Trump family comprised of -- the truths and lies, the hurts and joys, and basically everything that made them Trump. Most importantly, it dives into the life of Donald Trump and his siblings, revealing why and how he turned out to become the man he is.

If you have ever asked questions as to who Trump really is, or why he acts the way he does, then, this book is for you! A must read for everyone it is.

PART ONE: THE CRUELTY IS THE POINT

CHAPTER ONE: THE HOUSE

KEY TAKEAWAYS

- My grandparents' home was known as the *House.*
- Shortly after Mary got to the hospital, an emergency hysterectomy was performed on her.
- For young children to develop healthily, they have to be held and comforted as well as have their feelings acknowledged.

Maryanne screamed out to her dad, saying her mom was bleeding. My grandparents' home was known as the *House.* This was the very place they had lived in for less than a year. Despite having lived there for a while, it still felt very unfamiliar to them. Hence, when Maryanne found her mom in one of the bathrooms upstairs, unconscious, she became confused, instantly. The bathroom floor was covered in so much blood. Maryanne was so scared that instead of being overcome by her usual reluctance to disturb her father in his room, she immediately jumped to get him. Quickly, Fred got out of bed and finding his wife unresponsive, he ran to his bedroom and placed a call across to the hospital. Immediately, he was connected with someone who could get an ambulance to the House and ensure that the best doctors were waiting for them when they arrived at the hospital's emergency room.

Fred did all he could to explain the situation of things to the person at the other end. While the conversation ensued,

Maryanne heard her father use the word *menstruation*. At the time, it was strange to her. Mary was rushed to the hospital. Shortly after Mary got to the hospital, an emergency hysterectomy was performed on her. This was because doctors realized that she had developed severe postpartum complications which were not diagnosed after the birth of her son Robert, nine months earlier. The emergency hysterectomy resulted in an abdominal infection, causing further complications.

Back at home that day, Fred spoke on the phone with one of Mary's doctors for a short while. Afterward, he called Maryanne and informed her that the doctors said her mother would not make it through the night. A while later, while leaving for the hospital to be with his wife, he told Maryanne to go to school the next day, promising to call her if there were any changes. As young as she was, Maryanne understood what that meant. Her father just practically told her that he would call her if her mother died.

That night, Maryanne spent the greater part of the night in her room, crying. Her younger siblings were all asleep in their beds, completely unaware of all that had happened. The next day, she went to school, as her father instructed. She was so scared. While at school, her headmaster- Dr. James Dixon, came to get her as he mentioned to her that she had a call in his office. Mary was very convinced that her mother had passed. She was just twelve years of age, and all that ran across her mind was becoming a mother to her four younger ones.

She picked the phone up and heard her father say that her mother was going to make it. Mary did make it. In the next week, she had to undergo two more surgeries. Her road to recovery was a very long one, however. Over the course of the next six months, Mary was in and out of the hospital. Eventually, she developed severe osteoporosis owing to the sudden loss of estrogen that went with having her ovaries removed along with her uterus. This procedure was pretty standard at the time, but it was also very unnecessary. Owing to this, she was often in severe pain from unprompted fractures to her bones that never stopped thinning.

As children and babies, some of us were blessed to have had at least a parent who was emotionally available, consistently fulfilled all our needs, and gave us the attention we craved. For young children to develop healthily, they have to be held and comforted and have their feelings acknowledged. All of these come together to create a sense of security and safety, which allows these children to explore their world without excessive fear or anxiety that they cannot manage solely because they know they can always count on the lasting support of at least one caregiver.

Another critical part of a child's development is known as mirroring. Through this process, an attuned parent reflects processes and gives back to the baby's own feelings. When this process is skipped, children are significantly denied a vast amount of crucial information about how their minds work and how they can understand the world. In the same way a secure attachment to a primary caregiver can result in higher levels of emotional intelligence, mirroring remains the source of empathy.

From the very beginning, Mary and Fred were problematic parents. I do not recall my grandmother speaking to me about her parents, but I was aware that she was the youngest of ten children. In the early 1910s, she was raised in an often inhospitable environment. I'm not sure whether her own needs were sufficiently met as a child or not, but she was the kind of mother who comforted herself using her children, instead of comforting them. Her decision to attend to them was hinged on her own convenience, rather than when they needed her to do so. She was very needy and unstable. She also wallowed in a lot of self-pity, and more often than not, she put herself first. This was particularly true when it came to her boys- she always acted as if there were nothing she could do for them.

While she had to undergo surgeries, a void was created in her children's lives, both literally and emotionally. Things were hard enough, but because Maryanne, Elizabeth, and Freddy were quite grown, they could understand the happenings around their lives. To a reasonable extent, they could take adequate care of themselves. However, Donald and Robert were the worst hit. Donald was only two years old at the time, while Robert was nine months old. They were the most vulnerable of her children because no one else could fill the space the situation of things with her health had created. The housekeeper who lived with them was already overwhelmed with having to do so much. Their paternal grandmother made their meals, but she was very much like her son, Fred- physically unaffectionate and terse. In all truth, the five kids were motherless.

Mary was needy, Fred seemed devoid of emotional needs. Without mincing words, Fred was a huge sociopath. One would think that because Mary was unavailable because of her health, Fred would fill that gap and become the available parent for their kids. He didn't. He believed that dealing with kids was not his job, and would rather spend all his time at his job, as though his kids were capable of looking after themselves. To him, what was essential and needed his focus was his business.

CHAPTER TWO: THE FIRST SON

KEY TAKEAWAYS

- Freddy learned to love boating, fishing and waterskiing by spending time with his friends.
- Some of the Trump kids had come to adopt lying as a way of life.
- Whenever Freddy expressed a desire to own a pet, or simply joked around about it, Fred would retort, saying it was stupid.

As the oldest son in the family, Freddy's status had gone from having to protect himself from his father's terrible parental impulses to becoming a massive burden. As he continued to grow, he got torn between the responsibility that had been placed on him by his dad and his ordinary disposition to live life the way he wanted. His father, Fred, was in no way torn about this. In his opinion, Freddy ought to do one thing alone- spending time at the Trump Management office on Avenue Z, instead of hanging out with his friends in Peconic Bay. By the way, Freddy learned to love boating, fishing, and waterskiing by spending time with his friends.

By the time Freddy became a teenager, he knew very well what his father expected of him. He also knew he wasn't measuring up. It didn't take too long before his friends began to realize that Freddy became anxious and self-conscious around his father. Freddy and his friends often called Fred The Old Man. He never played with kids, being all stiff and formal around them. When Freddy got into his early teens, he began lying to his father about what his life looked like outside the house. The whole essence was to avoid the mockery the truth would bring upon him. He lied about everything- from what he did with his friends after school, to smoking. A particular incident happened where Freddy and his friend, Homer, stole a hearse for a joyride. Freddy pulled into a gas station to fill the vehicle tank up before returning it to the funeral home. His friend, Homer, was lying in the back. Just as Freddy pulled into the gas station, Homer sat up to see what it was like. Homer's action scared a man who was at the pump across from them. The man was convinced that he had just seen a corpse rising from the dead. Both Homer and Freddy laughed so hard until they cried. These were the kind of things Freddy lived for, but couldn't share with his father. Only when his father wasn't at home was he able to share his escapades with his siblings.

Some of the Trump kids had come to adopt lying as a way of life. In Freddy's case, lying was a defensive tool. For him, lying was much more than a means of circumventing his father's disapproval or avoiding punishment. Instead, it was a way of survival for him. For instance, Maryanne never defied her father's order out of a fear of being punished by being grounded or sent to her room. Donald, on the other hand, lied majorly to convince people that he was better than he was. For Donald, lying was a self-aggrandizement thing. These weren't the case for Freddy. If Freddy went against his father, the consequences were different, both in degree and kind. Hence, lying became his only defense against his father's efforts to defeat his natural sense of adventure, humor, and sensitivity.

11

Norman Vincent Peale was Fred's idol. Peale's ideas about inferiority complex shaped the harsh judgments that Fred held about Freddy. These ideas also gave him room to avoid taking responsibility for any of his kids. For Fred, weakness was the greatest sin anyone could fall into. He constantly worried that Freddy was going to turn out more like his own brother John, who, though wasn't unambitious, was interested in the wrong things like physics and engineering. These things, Fred found unimportant. He concluded that such softness could and should not be found in his own namesake, and by the time Freddy was ten, Fred was determined to toughen him up.

Whenever Freddy expressed a desire to own a pet or joke around, Fred would retort, saying that it was stupid. In so many ways, he made it evident that he hated when Freddy flinched, screwed up, or failed to decode what was expected of him. Worse still, he hated it even more that, when taken to task, Freddy apologized. Fred would mock him for apologizing. He desperately wanted his oldest son to become a killer in his parlance, but unfortunately, Freddy didn't even have a temperament suited for that.

What Fred wanted for his son was for Freddy to be invulnerable. When Fred's dad died, he appeared not to feel anything about his death. However, the suddenness of the event knocked him off balance as it took him by surprise. Years later, when he finally discussed it, he said that his father died, just like that, and that it did not seem real. He also mentioned not being that upset. However, he would get upset whenever he saw his mother crying and being sad. According to Fred, he felt sorrowful about his father's death from seeing his mother sad, not by his own feelings about what happened.

This was how Fred handled loss. He was able to move on by convincing himself that nothing particularly important had been lost. One thing Fred failed to realize, however, was that by ridiculing and questioning Freddy, he was creating a situation in which low self-esteem was almost inevitable. Fred was simultaneously telling his son that he had to be an unqualified success, and that he never could be. So, Freddy existed in a system that was all punishment, no reward. The other children, especially Donald, couldn't have helped but notice.

With all that was going on, Donald picked one lesson: that it was wrong to be like Freddy. Fred didn't respect his oldest son, so neither would Donald.

CHAPTER THREE: THE GREAT I-AM

KEY TAKEAWAYS

- Donald had seen enough of his older brother's struggles and his failure to meet up to their father's expectations.
- All of the time, Fred's attention was focused on just two things -- his business, and Freddy, his oldest son.
- Donald knew for a fact that he would never get to enjoy comfort or a soothing feeling, particularly at the points in his life when he needed them the most.

When Maryanne and Freddy left for their respective tertiary institutions of choice, Donald had seen enough of his older brother's struggles and his failure to meet up to their father's expectations. Truth be told, these things were very vague. One huge assumption that Fred carried about was that his subordinates knew what to do, even without being told. There was just one way to know if what you were doing was right: you didn't get dressed down for doing it.

It was one thing for Donald to avoid being in his father's bad books. It was an entirely different subject to get on his good sides. To achieve the latter, Donald ensured that he put to death any traits that he might have had in common with his older brother. Besides the fishing trip he, Freddy, and some of his friends went on, Donald became more of a country club and office person. The only grounds on which he differed from his father was that of golf. He also doubled down on the behaviors he had hitherto gotten away with; behaviors like bullying, pointing the finger, refusing to take responsibility, and disregarding authority.

According to Donald, by pushing back against his father, he earned his respect. However, in the real sense of things, Donald was only able to push back against his father because Fred let him. As a young child, Fred's attention was not focused on him. All of the time, Fred's attention was focused on just two things- his business, and Freddy, his oldest son. When Donald went off to military school at the age of thirteen, Fred began to appreciate Donald's disregard of authority. In general, Fred was a strict parent, but he accepted Donald's arrogance and bullying after he started noticing them. The only reason he was able to see them in the first place was that he identified with the same impulses.

Donald was continually encouraged by his father, and before long, he began to believe his own hype. By age twelve, he had a twitch on the right side of his mouth, which signaled an air of superiority. This was why Freddy began to refer to him as The Great I-Am.

Owing to the terrible conditions under which they were raised, Donald knew that he would never get to enjoy comfort or a soothing feeling, particularly at the points in his life when he needed them the most. For this reason, he decided that it was no use acting needy. Whether he knew it or not, neither of his parents was ever going to get to see the real him- who he was or who he might have been, for Mary was way too depleted to notice him, and Fred only took an interest in whichever of his sons had the most use to him. As a result, Donald naturally became whatever was most expedient. He developed a rigid personality to protect himself against pain and loss. However, this personality was not always positive. As much as it served as a form of protection for him, it denied him the ability to figure out how to trust people enough to get close to them.

Freddy was highly terrified of his father. He could not ask Fred for anything. Young Donald had watched and seen the results of Freddy's silence. In situations where Freddy took a different approach- a deviation from his father's often unspoken expectations, he ended up in humiliation and shame. Owing to this, Donald tried to do things differently. He chose to grovel himself with their father by ensuring that he smashed through every obstacle his older brother never dared. He knew how to play his cards well. Where Freddy flinched, Donald shrugged. He continually took the things he wanted without asking for permission. It wasn't as if Donald was brave. Instead, he did these things because he was afraid not to. It did not matter if Donald understood what the underlying message was, or not. Fred did. As far as Fred was concerned, both in life and family, there could only be one winner while everyone else had no choice but to lose. For years unending, Freddy tried so hard to do the right thing, but he kept failing at it. Unlike Freddy, however, Donald realized that there was nothing he could do that would be termed wrong, so he decided against trying to do anything right. He became a bolder and more aggressive person and was rarely challenged by the one person who mattered, his father. For some reason, Fred liked Donald's killer attitude, even though it played out as bad behavior.

Donald got worse. Even his mother, Mary, had no control over him, and Fred was hardly at home to see all these. Donald tormented his little brother, refused to do his chores, talked back, and never admitted he was wrong. He was never scared when he was told to wait until his father comes home. While that line worked magic on Freddy, it seemed more like a joke to Donald -- a joke that even his father seemed to be in on. This went on for a while, until 1959.

By 1959, Donald's misbehavior had hit the roof. While in school, he was reportedly known for fighting, bullying, and arguing with his teachers. Kew-Forest had had enough. Fred was on the school's board of trustees, causing Donald's actions to affect him in two different ways. Because of Fred, Donald's behavior was overlooked for much longer than it should have. However, these actions had escalated into physical arguments, which were becoming intrusive and time-consuming for him. Hence, when someone recommended that he send Donald to New York Military Academy, he didn't hesitate.

CHAPTER FOUR: EXPECTING TO FLY

KEY TAKEAWAYS

- In May 1964, Freddy flew his first official flight as a professional pilot from Boston's Logan Airport to LAX.
- Unlike all the others, Freddy put himself through flight school in college.
- As opposed to having all his decisions second-guessed and criticized by Fred, Freddy had all the controls on the flight deck.

No one, except the best pilots, were assigned to fly the Boston-Los Angeles route. In May 1964, Freddy flew his first official flight as a professional pilot from Boston's Logan Airport to LAX. This was less than six months after he had applied for a slot in the training class that year.

Within the Trump family, what Freddy achieved in the cockpit made him a unique person. No other child of Fred and Mary's could accomplish such a feat entirely by themselves. Maryanne came the closest to achieving this, having put herself through law school in the early 1970s and compiled a solid record as a prosecutor over nine years. However, she eventually got appointed at the federal appeals court mainly because Donald used his connections to favor her. Elizabeth worked for several decades in the job that Fred arranged for her at Chase Manhattan Bank. From the very beginning, Donald had been enabled, as each of his projects was funded and supported by Fred and other enablers. Up until now, this has remained the case. Besides a stint at a New York securities firm after graduating from college, Robert worked for Donald, before moving on to work for his father. Fred himself was not self-made. His mother started the business that became Trump Management.

Unlike all the others, Freddy put himself through flight school in college. He defied his father and had no support whatsoever from his entire family. To make matters worse, he enjoyed an active rain of contempt from them. Despite all obstacles, Freddy was determined to apply to TWA as many times as he would have to. On the very first try, he made it.

Back in the 1950s and 60's, a massive number of incoming pilots received their training in the military. Typically, a training class comprised of twenty students. From these twenty, four were each from the air force, navy, army, marines, and civilians. At the age of twenty-five, Freddy was one of the twelve men who got accepted into the airline's first 1964 pilot class. Ten out of these men had received their training in the military. There were no flight simulators at the time, meaning all their training was done in the air. This achievement was immense. Finally, Freddy began to reap the rewards of all the hours he had spent at the airfields while all his fraternity brothers partied.

At that time, traveling by air was at the peak of its shine. At the forefront of this glamour was Howard Hughes's Trans World Airlines- the favorite of the Hollywood rich and famous. TWA flew both domestically and internationally. The captain was God and treated accordingly, and thanks to

Hughes's penchant for beautiful women, the stewardesses all looked like movie stars.

The reactions that greeted pilots from passengers as they walked through the terminal -- the constant request for autographs and a host of other attention giving gestures were new to Freddy. They were a very welcome change from what he was used to at the Trump Management, where Freddy had struggled to gain respect. As opposed to having all his decisions second-guessed and criticized by Fred, Freddy had all the controls on the flight deck. Sadly, this wasn't enough for Fred. He made it clear to Freddy that he was embarrassed to have a bus driver in the sky for a son.

PART TWO: THE WRONG SIDE OF THE TRACKS

CHAPTER FIVE: GROUNDED

KEY TAKEAWAYS

- The life switch from New York Military Academy to College was a pretty tough transition for Donald.
- With the way things turned out between Freddy and Fred, Donald realized that he had the opportunity to become his father's right-hand man at Trump Management.
- In 1966, during the fall, Donald transferred from Fordham to the University of Pennsylvania.

Ever since September 1964, Donald had been living at the House. He commuted thirty minutes to Fordham University, driving his Bronx. The switch from life at the highly structured New York Military Academy to the liberal structure at college was a pretty tough transition for Donald. More often than not, he found himself at loose ends and ended up spending a whole lot of his time walking around the neighborhood in search of ladies to flirt with.

One particular afternoon, Donald came across Annamaria, who happened to be Billy Drake's girlfriend. She was standing in the driveway while she watched her father wash the car. Donald was well aware of who she was, but they had never gotten to speak. Annamaria knew all about Donald from Freddy. While both were chatting, she mentioned that she had attended a boarding school near New York Military Academy. Donald asked her which one it was, and when she told him, he replied, saying he was disappointed that she went to that school. Annamaria was three years older than Donald. Immediately, she asked him who he was to be disappointed in her. That was the end of the conversation. Donald's idea of flirting was majorly to insult her and act superior. This act struck Annamaria as juvenile, as though Donald were a second grader who found pulling a girl by her hair the only way to express his affection.

With the way things turned out between Freddy and Fred, Donald realized that he had the opportunity to become his father's right-hand man at Trump Management. Trump had learned to be the best, even in ways his father didn't intend. Donald was hell-bent on securing a degree befitting his new ambitions, even if all it got him were bragging rights. Fred did not know anything about the merits of one college over another college. He did not go to college, and neither did my grandmother. As a result, all of the Trump kids were on their own when it came to applying to schools. Donald was aware of the Wharton School's reputation and set his gaze on the University of Pennsylvania. Sadly, even though Maryanne did all of his homework, she couldn't write his tests. Donald always worried that his GPA would make it difficult for him to be accepted into Penn. He even enlisted the efforts of Joe Shapiro, who was a brilliant kid, by the way. Joe took his SATs for him. It was easy to do all these in those days because, at the time, there were no such things as photo IDs and computerized records. Donald paid Joe well. In a bid to ensure that he left nothing to chance, David requested help from his brother, Freddy. Freddy had a friend who worked in the admission office at Penn, James

Nolan. Donald asked Freddy to speak with Nolan, hoping Nolan would be willing to put in a good word for Freddy's kid brother. Freddy was happy to help Donald, even though he had intentions of his own. Freddy never saw Donald as a competition, but he also hated being around this sibling of his who was increasingly insufferable in every way. For Freddy, it was a relief to have Donald out of his way.

In the end, all of Donald's plans worked out. In all truth, all the strings Donald pulled may not even have been needed. Back in those days, Penn was much less selective than it is now. At the time, Penn accepted a half or more of its applicants. In any case, David got what he wanted. In 1966, during the fall, he transferred from Fordham to the University of Pennsylvania.

My grandfather completed the purchase of Steeplechase Park in July 1965, for the sum of 2.5 million dollars. A couple of months later, I was born. One year afterward, Trump Management was still struggling to get the approvals and zoning it needed to move ahead. They were also battling public opposition to the project.

Freddy mentioned to his friends that nothing had changed ever since his short stay at Trump Management. Fred, by constantly micromanaging and disrespecting Freddy, made what could have been an exciting challenge, a grim, joyless exercise. Failure was all that followed after, although Freddy still believed that if he had a hand in pulling the development off, he'd be on a much better footing with his father.

CHAPTER SIX: A ZERO-SUM GAME

KEY TAKEAWAYS

- My dad was aiming a rifle at my mom, and for some reason, he found it funny and kept laughing.
- Maryanne was in a lot of trouble.
- David often told Maryanne that his name would be known far and wide, far beyond even the reach of the Trumps.

I awoke to the sound of my dad's laughter. I didn't even know what time it was. My room was pretty dark, and the light from the hallway shone brightly through the underneath part of my door. I slipped out of bed. At the time, I was about two and a half years old, and my five-year-old brother was sleeping on the opposite end of the apartment. Alone, I went to peep and see what was going on.

Next to my room was my parents' room. The door to their room was wide open. All lights were turned on. I halted as I approached the threshold. Dad was standing, with his back turned to the chest of drawers, while my mom was sitting on the bed directly across from him. She was leaning away. One of her hands was held up, while the other hand supported her weight on the mattress. It took some time to understand what I was looking at. My dad was aiming a rifle at my mom, and for some reason, he found it funny and laughed.

My mom begged and begged him to stop. He continued to raise the gun until it was pointing at her face. She lifted her left arm higher and screamed again, more loudly. Dad seemed to find it funny. I turned and ran back to bed.

That night, my mother bundled my brother and me into the car and took us to a friend's house for the night. Finally, my father tracked us. He didn't seem to remember what he had done, or if he did at all, very vaguely. He, however, promised my mother that it would never happen again. By the time we returned to the apartment the next day, he was waiting for us. Himself and my mother both agreed that they would try to work things out. Sadly, they kept going through the motions of their marriage without making any attempts to acknowledge or fix the problems therein. Nothing would get better. Nothing would ever stay the same.

Less than two miles away, in another building owned by my grandfather, Maryanne was in a lot of trouble. Her husband, David, had lost a dealership -- a Jaguar dealership -- a couple of years before, and he still didn't have a job. If anyone paid attention, they would realize that all wasn't well, but all of Maryanne's siblings and even their friends just thought of Desmond as a joke. Freddy had never even understood the marriage in the first place; neither did he ever take his brother-in-law seriously.

Maryanne was twenty-two when she met David. She was then a graduate student at Columbia, studying public policy. Maryanne had planned to get a Ph.D. Still, because she wanted to avoid being shamed and called an old maid by everyone in her family, Freddy inclusive, she accepted David's proposal and dropped out of school after getting her master's degree.

The problem began when David, who was a catholic, insisted that Maryanne convert. Because she didn't want to upset her father or mother, she was afraid to ask for their blessing. Finally, she asked them, and all Fred said was that she should do whatever she wanted to do. She went on to explain how sorry she was to disappoint them.

David often told Maryanne that his name would be known far and wide, far beyond the Trumps' reach. Even though he was well educated, he did not have any apparent skills to support his ambition. Regardless, he was so convinced that he was going to find a way to succeed beyond his dreams and show them who he was. He was like the next big thing that never seemed to break through. Nothing ever materialized, and before long, he began drinking.

They lived in a rent-free Trump apartment, enjoying the same medical insurance as everyone else in the Trump family. However, free rent and medical insurance could not pay the bills, and they had no source of income. It remained a mystery as to why Maryanne was so financially dependent on her husband, Elizabeth lived in a gloomy one-bedroom apartment next to the 59th Street Bridge, Freddy was unable to buy a house, and his planes, boats and luxury cars continued to disappear. My grandparents had set up trust funds for all of Fred's kids in the 1940s. Hence, whether or not Maryanne was entitled to the principal yet, the trusts must have accrued some form of interest. However, because the three older children had been trained not to ever ask for anything, with their grandfather as the trustee of those trusts, they remain trapped in their financial circumstances. To them, by asking for help, you indirectly said that you were weak or greedy or were seeking an advantage over someone who needed nothing from you in return, although Donald was exempted from this line of thought.

After a few years, with David's situation remaining the same financially, Maryanne approached her mother in a nonsuspicious manner. She would casually say she needed some money for the laundry. In a bid to help retain her daughter's pride, her mother would hand her a can of quarters and dimes, which she took from my grandfather's buildings. Without these, Maryanne wouldn't have been able to feed herself or her son.

No matter how dire their situation was, the three oldest Trump children could not get anyone in their family to help them substantially. At some point, it seemed to be of no use trying at all. Maryanne was convinced that she was decorated with a badge of honor by refusing to request or receive help. Elizabeth accepted her lot as well, and my dad also came to believe it was what he deserved.

Things got worse with David Desmond. Left with no choice, Maryanne asked her father to offer David a place at Trump Management. Without asking if there were a problem, Fred offered his son-in-law a job as a parking lot attendant at one of his buildings in Jamaica Estates.

CHAPTER SEVEN: PARELLEL LINES

KEY TAKEAWAYS

- It didn't take too long before Freddy figured out that his father was not willing to create room for him nor delegate anything else to him but mundane tasks.
- Donald had bold ideas and the audacity to realize them.
- For Grandma, it was okay for her son to be rich and successful. However, she did not consider it okay for her son to show off.

When Freddy and Donald joined the Trump management in 1960 and 1968, they each had a similar expectation -- become their father's right-hand man, and succeed him afterward. At different times and in different ways, they had been groomed to fit that part. They never lacked the funds to buy expensive clothes or luxury cars. There ended the similarities between them.

It didn't take too long before Freddy figured out that his father was unwilling to create room for him or delegate him anything else but the mundane tasks. This was a problem that came to a peak at the height of the construction of Trump Village. Freddy felt trapped, unappreciated and miserable and so he left to find his success elsewhere. At twenty-five, he had become a professional pilot who was already flying the 707s for TWA and supporting his young family. This turned out to be the pinnacle of Freddy's personal and professional life. When he turned twenty-six and returned to Trump management, the imaginary chance for rehabilitation supposedly offered to him at Steeplechase evaporated, and soon, his prospects were at an end.

As at 1971, my dad had been working for my grandfather for eleven years, excluding ten months as a pilot. Despite this, my grandfather promoted Donald to Trump management's position at the age of twenty-four years. At the time, Donald had been on the job for only three years. He had minimal experience and way fewer qualifications. Somehow, Fred did not seem to mind.

The truth was that Fred did not need any of his sons at Trump Management. He had promoted himself to the firm's CEO, but nothing had changed about his job description. Fred was basically a landlord. Since the failure of Steeplechase six years ago, Fred had not been a developer. So, Donald's role as president was vague.

In the early 1970s, the federal government cut back on the FHA, so no more FHA funding was available to Fred. Mitchell-Lama, a New York State-sponsored program to provide affordable housing that funded Trump Village, also ground to a halt. Hence, it was pointless promoting Donald at a point like this. What exactly was he being promoted to do anyway? Fred had no development projects and no dependable political power structure. Worse still, New York City was neck-deep in financial constraints. The main reason why Fred promoted Donald was to shame and punish Freddy. In a long line of punishments, this was the latest. Indeed, it was the worst, particularly within the context in which it happened.

Fred was determined to get Donald a role. He had realized or was beginning to realize that even though Donald lacked the temperament needed for the day-to-day attention to detail that was required to run his business, Donald had something much more valuable. Donald had bold ideas and the audacity to realize them. For a long time, Fred had harbored aspirations to expand his business across the river into Manhattan, which was considered the Holy Grail of New York City real estate developers. Early on in his career, he had demonstrated that he had a knack for self-promotion, dissembling, and hyperbole. However, as the first-generation son of German immigrants, English was his second language. He needed to improve his communication skills. Therefore, he took the Dale Carnegie course for a reason, of which boosting his self-confidence wasn't a part. The course was a total failure. There was another obstacle, one which seemed even more challenging to overcome. Fred's mother, despite being forward-thinking, could also be very traditional. For her, it was okay for her son to be rich and successful. However, she did not consider it okay for her son to show off.

Donald did not have any restraint like that. And much as Fred did, he also hated Brooklyn. However, their reasons were pretty different. Donald hated Brooklyn for its lack of potential and the smallness of its working-class circle. He found it difficult to get out of there fast enough. Trump management was situated right in the heart of Brooklyn.

Besides being driven around Manhattan by a chauffeur paid by his father's company in a Cadillac leased by his father's company to scope out properties, Donald's job description included lying about his accomplishments and allegedly refusing to rent apartments to black people.

CHAPTER EIGHT: ESCAPE VELOCITY

KEY TAKEAWAYS

- The shoe was just one -- a gold shoe with a four-inch heel, totally filled with candy.
- For me, I was thankful the underwear would not expire.
- Once on holidays, Donald and Ivana came around the house driving an expensive car or a chauffeur-driven limo longer than my grandfather's.

I was seated at the dining table with the shoe right in front of me as I tried to figure out what its point was. I had taken my time to look through every box under the tree, hoping I'd find the other pair wrapped away, separately. I didn't find it. The shoe was just one- a gold shoe with a four-inch heel, filled with candy. The individual candy and the shoe itself were both wrapped in cellophane. I wondered where it came from.

Donald entered through the pantry. He was coming from the kitchen. He passed by me and asked what I was holding. I responded, saying it was a present from him. He stood surprised, after which he called out for his wife, Ivana. Responding to his call, she asked him what the matter was. He then told her that the shoe was great while he smiled. Perhaps, he thought that it was real gold.

All of these started in 1977 with my first present from Donald and his wife, Ivana. It was a three-pack of Bloomie's underwear, which retailed for twelve dollars. That same year, they gave Fritz a leather-bound journal. It felt like it was meant for someone older, but it was very nice, and I felt quite slighted until we realized that it was two years out of date. For me, I was thankful the underwear would not expire.

Once on holidays, Donald and Ivana came around the house, driving an expensive car or a chauffeur-driven limo longer than my grandfather's. They came into the foyer like socialites with Ivana dressed in furs and silk, voluminous hair, and makeup, while Donald was clad in costly three-piece suits and shiny shoes. Most times, everyone else was just conservatively dressed and unfashionable by comparison.

For a long time, I believed that Donald had broken out and built the business on his own. I also believed that my grandfather only cared about making and keeping money. These versions of the truth were very different. A New York Times article published on October 2, 2018, uncovered the vast amounts of alleged fraud and quasi-legal and illegal activities my family had engaged in for several decades.

In 1976, Roy Cohn suggested that Donald and Ivana sign a prenuptial agreement. At the time, Donald's father was his only source of income. Hence, the terms set for Ivana's compensation were based on Fred's wealth. From my grandmother, I heard that added to alimony and child support as well as the condo, Ivana insisted that the prenup included what Ivana described as a rainy day fund of one hundred and fifty thousand dollars. The divorce agreement between my parents also based on my grandfather's wealth. Still, Ivana's one hundred and fifty thousand dollars bonus was nearly twenty-one years of the six hundred dollars per month checks, which my mother received for child support and alimony.

Before Ivana entered the family, there was usually a sense of sameness to the holidays, which caused them to blur into one another. It was difficult to distinguish Christmas when I was five from what Christmas was like when I turned eleven. We never had to vary the routine. We'd enter the House through the front door at 1:00 p.m., dozens of packages in tow, handshakes, and air kisses all around, then gather in the living room for shrimp cocktail. Like the front door, we used the living room only twice a year.

As soon as Ivana became a part of the family, she joined Donald at the power center of the table. Donald always sat at my grandfather's right hand. Maryanne, Robert, and Ivana, who sat closest to them, formed a claque with one mission: to prop Donald up, follow his lead in the conversation, and defer to him as though nobody was as important as he was. Initially, I thought it was convenient. Early on, Maryanne and Robert had learned that there was no point in contradicting their father's apparent preference.

PART THREE: SMOKE AND MIRRORS

CHAPTER NINE: THE ART OF THE BAILOUT

KEY TAKEAWAYS

- The New York tabloids blared loudly with the headlines *Mary Trump Mugged.*
- Grandma mentioned that when Donald went to the Military Academy, she was relieved.
- According to Grandma, Donald never listened to her, and my grandfather didn't care.

The New York tabloids blared with the headlines "Mary Trump Mugged." Although I was fully aware of what happened, it still felt jarring to see the headlines every day as I passed through news kiosks on my way to the subway.

My grandmother wasn't only mugged. One kid grabbed her purse in the grocery parking store lot as she placed her shopping bags into her Rolls-Royce. The kid slammed her head against the car with a great deal of force that her brain hemorrhaged. She lost some sight as well as hearing. Upon hitting the pavement, her pelvis got fractured in several places. Her ribs broke as well. These injuries would have been much more severe if she didn't already have severe osteoporosis. When she arrived at Booth Memorial Hospital, her condition was so critical that we were not sure she would make it.

When she was moved out of the intensive care unit and into a private room, her level of progress became visible. The weeks that followed after, her pain became bearable. When her appetite began to return, I made and took whatever she wanted to her. One particular day, while she was drinking the butterscotch milkshake I brought her, Donald showed up.

He greeted both of us, and quickly kissed my grandmother, mentioning that she looked great. I told him that she was doing much better. My grandmother smiled at me, indicating to Donald that I had been visiting every day. Donald turned to me and said it must be nice to have a lot of free time on my hands. Grandma and I tried to hide our laughter. Grandma went on to ask him how he was faring, to which he responded, saying she shouldn't ask. For some reason, he seemed pretty upset.

My grandmother tried to stir up a conversation- asking him about the kids, and if anything was new with him and Ivana. He apparently was bored and didn't have so much to say. Ten minutes or so after, he left. When Grandma was sure that he was gone, she mentioned that he was cranky. At this point, I let out a laugh. I then told my grandmother that Donald was honestly having a tough time. In the space of the last twelve months, the Taj Mahal, his favorite Atlantic City casino, had declared bankruptcy just a little over a year after it had opened. Also, his marriage was a disaster, no thanks to his very public affair with Marla Maples. The banks had put him on an allowance, and worse, the paperback version of his second book, Surviving at the Top, had been published under the title "The Art of Survival."

Grandma seemed giddy, and I thought that the hospital staff might have to reduce her pain medications. She went on to say that Donald had always been like this. She mentioned that when he went to the Military Academy, she was so relieved. I asked her what she was able to do about Donald's increasing nonsense, but she asked me the same question again, rhetorically, though. According to Grandma, Donald never listened to her, and my grandfather didn't care. I was shocked because that didn't sound like my grandfather to me.

At the time, my grandfather was also in a hospital in Manhattan, getting a hip replacement. I honestly think he had only ever been in the hospital once- when he had a tumor on his neck near his right ear removed in 1989. I don't know if his hip surgery's timing was a mere coincidence or if it had been scheduled after my grandmother was admitted so she wouldn't have to deal with him while she recovered. For some time, his mental state had been deteriorating. While he was in the hospital, he had definitely taken a turn for the worse. Late at night on a few occasions, the nurses found him trying to leave wearing only boxer shorts. He told them he was going to find Mrs. Trump.

My Grandma seemed pretty happy not to be found.

CHAPTER TEN: NIGHTFALL DOES NOT COME AT ONCE

KEY TAKEAWAYS

- I had seen people whom my grandfather had known for years erased from his memory.
- In a matter of months, my grandfather went from habitually misplacing things and forgetting a word or a conversation here and there to forgetting familiar faces.
- You could practically measure what your worth to my grandfather was by how long he remembered you.
- I never heard him mention my dad in the years that followed his death.

We were at Mar-a-Lago. We sat at the very table where Donald, Marla, and I had lunch some years back. Easter had the family going there now. My grandfather turned to my grandmother, pointed to me, smiled, and asked who I was, describing me as a nice lady. He then turned to me and asked if I was a nice lady or not. I thanked him. My grandmother seemed upset, but I told her not to worry about it. I had seen people whom my grandfather had known for years erased from his memory. He could not remember most of his youngest grandchildren or his driver. This new nickname for me, Nice Lady, stuck. He called me a nice lady until his last sickness. He said it with such kindness and became particularly sweet to me after forgetting who I was.

Robert told my grandfather to come on, but he refused to move. He glanced at the crowd of people who had gathered at the gala thrown in both himself and my grandmother's honor. He had a look of panic over his face, as though he had no idea who anybody was or what he was doing up there. Until that point, I had only seen my grandfather look annoyed, contemptuous, amused, or self-satisfied. One other time when I saw my grandfather look unsettled was when occasion Donald had taken him to play golf. My grandfather had no use for pastimes. I was at the house when they both returned, and I nearly didn't recognize my grandfather. Both men were clad in golf clothes, with my grandfather wearing light blue pants, a white cardigan, and matching white shoes. In my entire life, it was the first time I got to see my grandfather dressed in something else besides a suit. He had never looked so uncomfortable and self-conscious as he did that day.

In a matter of months, my grandfather went from habitually misplacing things and forgetting a word or a conversation here and there to forgetting familiar faces. You could practically measure what your worth to my grandfather was by how long he remembered you. I don't know if he even remembered my dad. I never heard him mention my dad in the years that followed his death.

Maryanne made sure that my cousin, David, who was a clinical psychologist at the time, went with my grandfather to all of his appointments for checkups and neurological exams in a determined effort to ensure he was cemented in my grandfather's memory. It didn't take long before my grandfather referred to David as the doctor.

I was at Mar-a-Lago, standing at the pool with my grandfather and Maryanne when he pointed to me and asked Maryanne if I was a nice lady. It was over a year since my grandpa started referring to me as Nice Lady, Maryanne replied in the affirmative, saying I was a nice lady. My grandfather then looked at her carefully and asked who she was. Her eyes watered as if somebody had slapped her. Gently, she told him who she was. She was Maryanne. He smiled, but the name didn't mean anything to him anymore.

He never forgot Donald.

CHAPTER ELEVEN: THE ONLY CURRENCY

KEY TAKEAWAYS

- On the 25th of June, 1999, Fred Trump passed on.
- My grandfather's favorite poem was read by Elizabeth.
- When the service was over, the six oldest grandchildren escorted the casket to the hearse as honorary pallbearers.

On the 25th of June, 1999, Fred Trump passed on. The day after, his obituary got published in the New York Times. The article was titled Fred C. Trump, Postwar Master Builder of Housing for Middle Class, Dies at 93. The obituary writer contrasted Fred's status as a self-made man with Donald, whom he described as a flamboyant son. My grandfather had a propensity for picking up unused nails at his construction sites and handing them over to his carpenters the next day. The writer ensured that this information was noted before giving the details of my grandfather's birth.

The Times also repeated the familiar line that Donald built his business with very little help from my grandfather. This little help was described as a small amount of money. We all sat in the library, with a copy of the Times each in our hands. Robert was scolded by his siblings for telling the Times that my grandfather's estate was worth between two hundred and fifty million and three hundred million dollars. Maryanne warned him never to give out numbers, lecturing him as though he were a stupid kid. Robert just stood there, ashamed, cracking his knuckles and bouncing his feet, just like my grandfather. Robert's evaluation of the business empire was ridiculously low, for we would eventually come to know that it was worth four times more. For what it was worth, Maryanne and Donald would have never admitted that it was that much.

Later on, we all stood upstairs in the Madison Room at the Frank E. Campbell Funeral Chapel on Manhattan's Upper East Side. This was the most private and luxurious bereavement service provider in the city. We smiled and shook hands as a seemingly endless line of visitors passed through. There were more than eight hundred persons who passed through the rooms. While some were there to pay their respects, others were there to catch a glimpse of Donald.

The day of the funeral came. Marble Collegiate Church was filled to its ultimate capacity. From the beginning of the service, until it ended, everyone played one role or the other. The entire ceremony was well choreographed. Elizabeth read my grandfather's favorite poem. All the remaining siblings gave eulogies, alongside my brother, who spoke on my dad's behalf. My cousin, David, represented the grandchildren. Mostly, they told stories about my grandfather, although, in all of it, my brother was the only one who came close to humanizing him. For the most part, they all emphasized my grandfather's material success, instincts, and talent for savings. The only person who deviated from the script was Donald. Somehow, his eulogy became a talk about his own greatness. It was so embarrassing that Maryanne later told David not to allow any of her siblings to speak at her funeral.

When the service was over, the six oldest grandchildren escorted the casket to the hearse as honorary pallbearers. This meant that others did the heavy lifting while we got the credit. This was often the case in our family.

From Fifth Avenue and 45th Street to the Mid-Town Tunnel, all the streets had been closed to cars and pedestrians, making our motorcade, which came with a police escort slide out of the city, easily. Without the traffic and blocks, it was a quick trip to the burial held at the All Faiths Cemetery in Middle Village, Queens.

After the burial, we returned to the city as quickly as we could. By this time, the fanfare had significantly reduced. We had lunch at Donald's apartment, after which I accompanied my grandmother back to the house. The two of us sat in the library and chatted for a while. She seemed tired but relieved. It had been a very long day; a very long few years, actually. Other than the live-in maid, who was asleep upstairs, it was just the two of us. I was supposed to be on my honeymoon. I stayed with her until she was ready to go to bed.

The will was finally brought to us. We got nothing!

CHAPTER TWELVE: THE DEBACLE

KEY TAKEAWAYS

- In the world of my family, money was the only thing that mattered.
- Jack was an arrogant man who agreed to have us as his clients.
- Laurino made a defense case for the cancellation of the insurance by claiming at first that we had no right to expect the insurance in perpetuity.
- My father and his whole line had now been successfully removed.

I sat, holding my phone in my hand, unsure of what to do next. It was one of those moments that changes everything -- what came before and what will come after? It was all too much for me to process. I called my brother, and as soon as I heard his voice, I burst into tears.

Fritz called my grandmother to see if he could explain what we were asking for, but they basically had the same conversation. She ended things with him on a slightly different note, though. She mentioned that when our father died, he didn't have two nickels to rub together. In the world of my family, that was the only thing that mattered. If your only currency is money, that's the only lens through which you determine worth. With someone like my father, who had accomplished very little in that context, my father was worth nothing—regardless of whether he was their son. Furthermore, since my father died penniless, his children were not entitled to anything.

My grandfather had the right to change his will as it suited him. My uncles and aunts also had the right to follow his instructions to the letter, even though none of them deserved a share of my grandfather's fortune any more than my dad did.

We took Irwin's advice and approached Jack Barnosky. Jack was a partner at Farrell Fritz, the largest law firm in Nassau County. Jack was an arrogant man who agreed to have us as his clients. He had a strategy in mind, and it was to prove that my grandfather's 1990 will should be overturned, claiming that at the time the will was signed, Fred Trump was not of sound mind, and he had been under the undue influence of his children.

Less than a week after we served the executors, Jack received a letter from Lou Laurino, a lawyer representing my grandfather's estate. The medical insurance which the Trump Management provided us since we were born had just been revoked. The insurance covered everyone in the Trump family. My brother had relied on this insurance to pay for my nephew's overwhelming medical expenses. When William took ill the first time, Robert promised Fritz that they would take care of everything and that all Fritz had to do was send the bills to the office.

Taking our insurance away, which was Maryanne's idea, was of no benefit whatsoever to them. It only served the purpose of causing us more pain and desperation. By that time, William was already out of the hospital. However, he was still prone to seizures. These seizures have put him in a state of cardiac arrest so severe that he would not have survived without CPR, more than once.

The entire family knew this, but no one objected. Not even my grandmother, who was fully aware of the expensive medical care that her great-grandchild would need for the rest of his life. Fritz and I had no choice but to launch another lawsuit to make them reinstate William's medical insurance. The suit required depositions and affidavits from the doctors and nurses responsible for William's care. It was time-consuming and stressful and culminated in an appearance in front of a judge.

Laurino made a defense case for the cancellation of the insurance by claiming at first that we had no right to expect the insurance in perpetuity. He claimed that instead, it was a gift my grandfather bestowed upon us out of the goodness of his heart. He watered down William's condition, claiming that the nurses who watched him around the clock were overpriced baby sitters. He topped it all by saying that if Fritz and Lisa were worried that their infant son might have another seizure, they should just learn CPR.

My grandmother died soon after. I did not get to see her. Fritz and I decided to attend Gam's funeral, but knowing we were unwelcome, we stood in one of the overflow rooms at the back of Marble Collegiate Church. Along with a couple of Donald's security guards, we watched the service on a closed-circuit monitor.

I received a copy of my grandmother's will a few weeks after her death. It was exactly like my grandfather's. It was even worse, with my brother and I removed from the section outlining the bequests for her grandchildren.

My father and his entire line had now been successfully removed.

PART FOUR: THE WORST INVESTMENT EVER MADE

CHAPTER THIRTEEN: THE POLITICAL IS PERSONAL

KEY TAKEAWAYS

- Almost ten years went by before I saw my family again.
- It was relieving to discover that things were pleasant and civil between us.

Almost ten years went by before I saw my family again. I finally got to see them in October 2009 when my cousin, Ivanka, married Jared Kushner. I had no idea why I got the invitation.

As the limousine I took from my home on Long Island approached Donald's golf club in New Jersey, I didn't know what to expect. The ushers around handed out black shawls, making me feel a little less exposed as I wrapped one around my shoulders.

The outdoor event held under a large white tent. Gilt chairs lined up in rows on either side of a gilt-trimmed runway carpet. Donald stood in a yarmulke, awkwardly. Before the vows, Jared's father, Charles, who was released from prison three years before, rose to inform us that when Jared introduced him to Ivanka, he had thought that she would never be good enough to become a part of his family. Only after she committed to converting to Judaism and worked hard to make it happen, did he begin to think she might be worthy of them after all. Considering the fact that Charles had been convicted of several crimes, I found his condescension out of line. When the ceremony was over, my brother, his wife, and I entered the clubhouse.

While walking down the hallway, I saw Uncle Rob. The last time I had spoken with him was in 1999 when he hung the phone up on me after I mentioned to him that Fritz and I were hiring a lawyer to contest my grandfather's will. As I approached him, I was shocked to see him break into a smile. He even greeted me in the typical Trump style. We spent a couple of minutes exchanging pleasantries. Having been done with him, I walked up the stairs, where I spotted Donald and walked towards him. We exchanged greetings, and he kissed my cheek, just like Rob had. It was relieving to discover that things were pleasant and civil between us.

CHAPTER FOURTEEN: A CIVIL SERVANT IN PUBLIC HOUSING

KEY TAKEAWAYS

- My grandfather viewed Donald as a vanity project funded at the expense of more worthy pursuits.
- Donald was used, despite his constant failures and lack of judgement, as the public face of his own derailed ambition.
- In the first forty years of my grandfather's real estate career, he never acquired debts.

From the House to the Trump tower triplex to the West Wing, there is a through line. The same exists from Trump Management to the Trump Organization to the Oval Office. The former are mainly controlled environments within which Donald's material needs have always been cared for. The latter are a series of sinecures where the work was done by others, causing Donald to never need to acquire the expertise to attain or retain power. In a partial way, this explains Donald's disdain for others' expertise.

All these shielded Donald from all his failures, thereby resulting in him believing in himself as a success.

My grandfather viewed Donald as a vanity project funded at the expense of more worthy pursuits, the same way Donald viewed the border wall. Fred didn't groom Donald to succeed him. Instead, Donald was used despite his constant failures and lack of judgment, as the public face of his own derailed ambition. Fred kept supporting Donald's unfounded sense of accomplishment until the only gift

Donald possessed was the ability to be hoodwinked by greater and more powerful men.

A lot of people were willing to use and take advantage of Donald. Journalists and gossip columnists in the 1980s discovered that Donald could not tell the difference between mockery and flattery and then used his shamelessness to market more papers. That image, and the weakness of the man (Donald) it portrayed appealed to Mark Burnett.

In the first forty years of my grandfather's real estate career, he never acquired debts. In the '70s and '80s, all of that changed as Donald's ambition grew, and he continued to misstep. Without Fred's influence and money, Trump could never have been accomplished. By the late 1980s, however, the Trump Organization seemed to be in the business of losing money, as Donald siphoned untold millions away from Trump Management to support the growing myth of himself as a real estate Phenom and master dealmaker.